Holiday Entertaining

Irresistible Recipes for the Holiday Season

by Polly Clingerman

AMERICAN ★COOKING★ GUILD

Boynton Beach, Florida

Dedication
For John

Acknowledgments
—Cover Design and Layout by Pearl & Associates, Inc.
—Cover Photo by Burwell and Burwell
—Edited by Marian Levine
—Food Styling by Claudia Burwell

Revised Edition 1997
Copyright © 1991 by Polly Clingerman
All rights reserved.
Printed in U.S.A.
ISBN 0-942320-28-X

More...Quick Recipes for Creative Cooking!
The American Cooking Guild's *Collector's Series* includes over 30 popular cooking topics such as Barbeque, Breakfast & Brunches, Chicken, Cookies, Hors d' Oeuvres, Seafood, Tea, Coffee Pasta, Pizza, Salads, Italian and many more. Each book contains more than 50 selected recipes For a catalog of these and many other full sized cookbooks, send $1 to the address below and a coupon will be included for $1 off your first order.

Cookbooks Make Great Premiums!
The American Cooking Guild has been the premier publisher of private label and custom cookbooks since 1981. Retailers, manufacturers, and food companies have all chosen The American Cooking Guild to publish their premium and promotional cookbooks. For further information on our special market programs, please contact the address below.

The American Cooking Guild
3600-K South Congress Avenue
Boynton Beach, FL 33426

Table of Contents

Breads, Pastry & Cakes

Cookies

Candy

Beverages

Introduction

Holidays, with their rich traditions, are our opportunities to become memory makers as we recreate our heritage, pass it on to our children, and share it with friends.

Food fills a big, warm place in holiday seasons—the spicy smells of baking, the crisp golden bird with its herbed stuffing, the nogs and glögg, the cookies and cakes. A holiday cookbook is really a treasury of those memories: of good things past and good things to come, and in that spirit I offer this collection of traditional treats and a few splendid novelties. I hope you will use it with pleasure.

Holidays are a time to entertain, and parties should be fun, not a frenzied race down to the wire. If you have found holidays too hectic in the past, don't cut down on what you do; instead, make it easier. You can. Plan ahead—it is never too early. Get everything off your mind and onto paper: lists of decorations, guests, groceries. Make a timetable.

Keep a batch of cookie dough in the refrigerator ready to bake fresh when callers drop in. And don't forget to remember friends with pretty boxes of cookies and candies from your own kitchen.

You can't really overdo things at the holidays. Abundance is part of the season. Set out bowls of nuts and candies. Tie bright bows around newel posts. And use candles with abandon—tall ones, fat ones, candles in glass cups. Nothing creates so festive and cosy an atmosphere for parties as candlelight. Dig out every shiny table ornament you have—gold, silver, brass, glass. Holiday tables should sparkle.

Consider a dinner centerpiece of a basket of tiny gifts, each with a long ribbon attached. Everyone pulls a ribbon end to find his gift. The children will be enchanted.

Remember that holidays are a time of joy, not frenzy. As you write the invitations; as you stir and broil and baste and boil; add generous pinches and sprinkles of joy. Your delight in the season is your gift to family and friends, the magic ingredient that will make your home and parties sparkle.

Happy Holidays!

Three Suggested Menus

A Traditional Family Dinner

Roast Turkey with All the Trimmings
Peas with Pecans
Old Fashioned Creamed Onions
Creamy Buffet Mashed Potatoes
Southern Holiday Sweet Potatoes
Gail's Jellied Cranberry Salad

An Elegant Dinner

Scandinavian Eggs Mayonnaise
Glazed Cornish Game Hens with Wild Rice Stuffing
Gala Green Bean Salad
Holly Berry Mint and Chocolate Pie

A Holiday Buffet

Beef Stroganoff
Holiday Seafood Casserole
Fluffy White Rice
Revelers's Spinach Casserole
Romaine Salad with Orange-Almond Dressing
Holiday Baked Cranberry Pudding
Classic Pumpkin Pie

APPETIZERS

Quichlettes

Luscious little tarts of cheese, salami and onion. Make them ahead and reheat, or freeze for longer storage.

```
          pastry for 2 9-inch crusts
 1 1/3    cups coarsely grated Cheddar cheese
  2/3     cup salami, chopped fine
  1/3     cup green onions, chopped fine
   4      eggs, slightly beaten
 1 1/3    cups sour cream
   1      teaspoon salt
   1      teaspoon Worcestershire sauce
```

Preheat oven to 375°.

Roll pastry very thin (about 1/16-inch) and cut in rounds, Fit into 24 2 1/2-inch muffin pans.

Combine cheese, salami and onion. Put an equal amount in each lined muffin pan. In a small bowl mix eggs, sour cream, salt, and Worcestershire sauce. Place a generous tablespoonful in each tart. Bake the tarts at 375° for 20 to 25 minutes or until pastry is brown and filling is set.

Note: If you make the tarts in the morning, reheat them at 350° for 8 to 10 minutes. If reheating from frozen state increase time to 10 to 12 minutes.

Yield: 24.

Blue Cheese-Nut Log

With this wonderful standby in the refrigerator or freezer you're always ready to entertain.

8   ounces blue cheese, room temperature
8   ounces cream cheese, room temperature
4   ounces butter, room temperature
1   Tablespoon shallots or spring onions, chopped
1   Tablespoon brandy or cognac
1   cup finely chopped pecans

Cream cheeses with butter until well mixed. Mix in shallots and brandy. Form the mixture into a long roll and coat the outside with chopped nuts. Chill in the refrigerator or wrap in plastic and freeze until ready to use. (If frozen, let defrost for 45 minutes before serving.) Serve chilled or at room temperature with warmed crackers or thinly sliced French bread.

Yield: about 2½ cups.

Shrimp Dip

For a delicious change, serve this spicy dip hot—heating makes the cream cheese oozy and luscious tasting.

8   ounces cream cheese, room temperature
1   Tablespoon curry powder
¼   teaspoon garlic powder
¼   cup mango chutney, chopped fine
1   cup cooked shrimp, cut in small pieces
½   cup sour cream
2   Tablespoons milk

In a medium bowl mix cream cheese with curry, garlic powder and chutney. Stir in shrimp, sour cream and enough milk to make a nice dipping consistency. Serve at room temperature or gently heated. Use dippers such as crackers, melba toast and raw vegetables.

Yield: about 2¾ cups.

Fluffy Cheese Puffs

People can get rather emotional about these seductive morsels. A member of my family was quite cross to learn that I had thrown out the last three after a holiday party—her mouth was still watering the next day! Keep a bag of them in the freezer to bake fresh when well-wishers drop in.

> 4 ounces cream cheese
> 1/2 cup butter
> 4 ounces cheddar cheese, cubed
> 3 egg whites
> 1 loaf (1 pound) of unsliced white bread, crust removed

Melt cream cheese, butter and cheddar cheese in a pan either over hot water or over very low heat, stirring until smooth. Cool to lukewarm.

Beat egg whites stiff and fold into the cooled cheese mixture.

Cut the bread into 1-inch cubes. Dip each cube into the cheese mixture, using a fork, and swirl it around to coat completely. Often you have to spread the cheese mixture on the bread with a knife. Place on greased cookie sheet and refrigerate overnight. (Or freeze at this point and store frozen cubes in plastic bags.)

Preheat oven to 400°.

Bake cheese puffs on a greased cookie sheet for about 8 minutes or until they start to brown delicately. Serve hot.

Yield: 5 1/2 dozen.

Pâté Royale

Rich, smooth, delicious. Make it in a minute, savor it at leisure.

> 1 cup (2 sticks) butter, slightly softened
> 1 can (4 ounces) liver pâté
> few grinds cracked black pepper
> 2 Tablespoons Calvados or Cognac (or Madeira or Sherry)

In a small bowl beat butter fluffy with an electric mixer. Beat in the liver pâté, pepper and Calvados. Chill it well.

Delicious as is, or—my favorite trick—hollow out small French rolls from the end, stuff them with the pâté and chill. Slice very thin.

Yield: about 1½ cups.

Golden Olives

Fat little olives baked in buttery, cheesy pastry. Hot and bewitching.

> 1 cup grated sharp Cheddar cheese
> 2 Tablespoons butter, room temperature
> ½ cup flour
> dash cayenne pepper
> 24 small to medium pimento-stuffed olives

Preheat oven to 400°.

In a small bowl cream the cheese and butter. Add flour and cayenne, blending well. Mold a teaspoonful of dough around each olive, covering it completely. Place on baking sheet and bake at 400° for 15 minutes or until pastry is golden.

Yield: 24.

Hot Zucchini Squares

Very good with drinks, and they're also a wonderful contrast to the sweets at afternoon teas and morning coffees.

      3 cups zucchini, very thinly sliced
    1/4 cup minced onion
      2 Tablespoons parsley
    1/2 teaspoon oregano
    3/4 teaspoon salt
      1 clove garlic, minced
    1/2 cup grated Parmesan cheese
      4 eggs, slightly beaten
      1 cup flour
  1 1/2 teaspoons baking powder
    1/2 teaspoon seasoned salt
    1/8 teaspoon black pepper
      1 Tablespoon melted butter
    1/2 cup vegetable oil

In a large bowl mix zucchini, onion, parsley, oregano, salt, garlic and cheese. Stir in eggs and mix well. In a small bowl combine flour, baking powder, seasoned salt and pepper. Mix well into the zucchini mixture, then add melted butter and oil. Pour into a greased 13x9x2-inch casserole and bake at 350° for 25 minutes or until golden. Cut in squares and serve warm.

This freezes well.

Yield: about 4 dozen squares.

Scandinavian Eggs Mayonnaise

Here is an elegant, sophisticated, utterly seductive first course for your most glamorous dinner: eggs mayonnaise with smoked salmon and caviar.

4	hard cooked eggs
2	Tablespoons mayonnaise
	salt and pepper to taste
4	slices smoked salmon
8	2-inch circles close-textured white bread (2 to 3 slices bread)
$1/4$	cup mayonnaise
$1/4$	cup sour cream
$1^1/2$	teaspoons lemon juice
$1/2$	to 1 teaspoon dried dill weed (or to taste)
2	Tablespoons (1 ounce) caviar

Halve the eggs and press the yolks through a sieve. Mash them with 2 tablespoons mayonnaise and season to taste with salt and pepper. Fill the whites with this mixture.

Place a round of smoked salmon, cut to fit, on each bread circle. Top with an egg half, filled side down. Place on small serving plates.

In a small bowl mix mayonnaise, sour cream, lemon juice and dill. Add salt if needed. Pour sauce equally over eggs. Top each with a small spoonful of caviar. Serve immediately.

Yield: 8 servings.

SALADS

Celestial Fruit Salad

A treasured recipe from the forties. A wonderful, unsophisticated, dreamy, creamy mixture of grapes and pineapple and half-melted marshmallows, folded into a tart, lemon custard dressing.

2   cans (1 pound 4-ounces each) sliced pineapple, drained
4   egg yolks
    juice of 2 lemons
1   teaspoon sugar
1/2 teaspoon salt
1   cup whipping cream
1   package (1 pound) bite-size marshmallows
2   pounds red grapes, halved and seeded
2   Tablespoons sugar

Drain the pineapple and cut it into bite-size pieces. Set aside.

In a double boiler mix egg yolks, lemon juice, sugar and salt. Cook over boiling water until the mixture is thick, about 10 to 15 minutes. Cool. Whip the cream and fold it into the yolk mixture.

Place pineapple, marshmallows and grapes in a large, noncorrodable bowl. Fold dressing into the fruit mixture along with 2 tablespoons of sugar. Cover and chill in the refrigerator for 24 hours. During this time the marshmallows will partially melt into the custard, sweetening it a bit. Just before serving, taste. If it needs more sweetness add another tablespoon sugar.

Yield: 12 servings.

Mimosa Cauliflower Salad

A beautiful centerpiece for a holiday buffet.

> 1 large cauliflower
> 2 cups water
> 2 teaspoons lemon juice
> 1 teaspoon salt
> 2 Tablespoons chives or parsley
> 1/2 cup spring onions, chopped
> 8 hard cooked eggs, finely chopped
> 4 teaspoons Dijon mustard
> 2 teaspoons seasoned salt
> 1 1/2 cups salad oil
> 1/2 cup white wine vinegar

Leave the cauliflower head whole, but remove all green leaves. In a large pot bring 2 cups of water to a boil, and add lemon juice, salt and the cauliflower. Simmer uncovered for 10 to 20 minutes, until the cauliflower is just crisp-tender. Remove, drain, and cool to lukewarm.

In a medium bowl whisk together chives, spring onions, chopped eggs, mustard, seasoned salt, oil and vinegar.

Place the cauliflower on a lettuce-lined platter. Pour half the sauce over it, taking care to coat completely and uniformly. Refrigerate for at least 2 hours so the flavors will penetrate. Serve chilled or at room temperature. Serve the remaining sauce separately.

Yield: 6 servings.

Gala Green Bean Salad

Green beans and mushrooms bathed in a mustard vinaigrette dressing. Perfect for the busy holidays because you make it up to a day ahead.

2   Tablespoons white wine vinegar
1¹/2   teaspoons Dijon mustard
¹/4   cup olive oil
2   Tablespoons salad oil
¹/2   teaspoon dried dillweed
    salt and pepper to taste
1   minced green onion, white and green
12   ounces fresh green beans, washed and trimmed
8   ounces raw mushrooms, sliced thickly
1   hard cooked egg, finely chopped

In a small bowl whisk together vinegar, mustard, oil, dillweed, minced green onion, salt and pepper. Set aside.

Add beans to a large pot of boiling, salted water and cook at a rolling boil for 8 minutes or until crisp-tender. Drain the beans, pat dry with paper towels, place in a bowl and immediately, while they are still hot, mix with the dressing. Chill at least 4 hours, or overnight, in the refrigerator.

Just before serving clean the mushrooms, slice thickly and toss with the salad. Sprinkle the top with chopped egg and serve at room temperature.

Yield: 6 servings.

Gail's Jellied Cranberry Salad

A holiday tradition in my niece's household, this bright red fruit and nut mold is a perfect accompaniment for roast fowl, ham or pork.

> 1 *package (6 ounces) raspberry gelatin*
> 2 *cups boiling water*
> 1 *cup cold water*
> ³/4 *cup reserved pineapple juice*
> 1 *can (1 pound, 4 ounces) crushed pineapple, drain and reserve juice*
> 1 *cup fresh red grapes, halved and seeded*
> 1 *cup walnuts, coarsely chopped*
> 1 *cup celery, chopped medium fine*
> 1 *can (1 pound) cranberry sauce*

In a medium bowl dissolve gelatin in boiling water. When the liquid is clear, add cold water and ³/4 cup of the pineapple juice. Stir in grapes, pineapple, walnuts and celery and refrigerate until the mixture has thickened to the consistency of unbeaten egg whites. Stir in the cranberry sauce and spoon into a 12 cup mold (if you use a 13x8-inch cake pan you can cut it into squares). Chill until firm.

Yield: 10 to 12 servings.

Romaine Salad with Oranges

This salad couples oranges with crisp Romaine and another Middle-East exotic, the almond.

2   Tablespoons olive oil
6   Tablespoons peanut oil
$^1/_4$ cup tarragon vinegar
$1^1/_4$ teaspoons grated orange rind
$1^1/_2$ teaspoons sugar
$^1/_2$ teaspoon dried tarragon
$^1/_4$ teaspoon garlic salt
$^1/_8$ teaspoon pepper
     dash Tabasco®
2   medium heads Romaine lettuce (about 6 cups torn)
1   large red onion, sliced thinly
1   can (11 ounces) mandarin oranges, drained
1   avocado, sliced
$^1/_2$ cup slivered almonds

In a small bowl whisk together oils, vinegar, orange rind, sugar, tarragon, garlic salt, pepper and enough Tabasco to give the dressing a clean edge. Cover and chill for 30 minutes or more, to let the flavor develop.

Mix Romaine, onion, mandarin oranges and avocado in a large salad bowl. Just before serving, give the dressing a good stir and toss it well with the salad. Sprinkle with almonds.

Yield: 6 servings.

VEGETABLES

Southern Sweet Potatoes

This heady mixture of spice and cream and butter will glorify a ham, a roast or chops at any season. People do tend to scrape their plates clean when served this dish.

> 6 *sweet potatoes or yams (approximately 6 to 7 ounces each)*
> *1/3 cup butter, room temperature*
> *1/2 cup brown sugar, firmly packed*
> *1/2 cup table cream or evaporated milk*
> *1/3 cup bourbon*
> *1/2 teaspoon cinnamon*
> *1/4 teaspoon nutmeg*
> *salt to taste*
> *1/3 cup chopped pecans, sautéed in 1/2 Tablespoon butter*

Boil potatoes until tender (about 30 minutes if left whole). Remove the skins and mash. Beat in the butter, sugar, cream, bourbon, cinnamon, nutmeg and salt. Add more cream if needed to make a soft, creamy mixture. Taste and adjust seasonings. Serve hot topped with sautéed pecans.

Yield: 8 servings.

Peas with Pecans

A festive way to serve peas.

    2   packages (10 ounces each) frozen peas
    6   Tablespoons butter
  $1/2$ teaspoon celery salt
  $3/4$ cup pecan halves

Cook peas according to package directions. Drain and return to the pan. In a small saucepan melt the butter. Add celery salt and pecans and sauté until pecans are lightly toasted. Pour over peas and mix well. Reheat briefly if necessary. Serve hot.

Yield: 8 servings.

Revelers'Spinach Casserole

This wonderful dish has turned spinach haters into spinach fans. The texture is marvelous; almost like a fallen soufflé, and oh, the lovely creamy, cheesy flavor.

    5   to 6 Tablespoons butter
    8   ounces American cheese
    6   eggs
    6   Tablespoons flour
    1   quart (4 cups) small curd cottage cheese
    3   packages (10 ounces each) frozen spinach, thawed

Preheat oven to 350°.

Cut butter and cheese in ¼-inch cubes. Set aside. In a medium mixing bowl beat eggs lightly. Add flour, cottage cheese, butter and American cheese. Squeeze spinach as dry as possible and add. Mix well. Place in a greased 9x13-inch ovenproof dish and bake at 350° for 1 hour. Serve hot.

Yield: 8 servings.

Creamy Buffet Mashed Potatoes

Mashed potatoes are always a bother because you usually can't make them ahead. But these you not only can make ahead, you can freeze them! And they are delicious.

    4   *large baking potatoes (approximately 10 ounces each)*
    1   *package (8 ounces) cream cheese, diced and at room temperature*
    1   *medium onion, finely chopped*
    3   *eggs*
    3   *Tablespoons flour*
    1   *teaspoon salt*
  $1/4$ *teaspoon pepper*
    2   *Tablespoons butter*

Wash potatoes and bake at 400° for about 40 minutes, or until done. Halve them and scoop out the insides. (Reserve skins for another use or use as described in the variation below.)

Put the potatoes through a ricer into a large bowl (or grate them). Add cream cheese and beat smooth with mixer at medium speed. Add onion, eggs, flour, salt and pepper and beat smooth. Spoon the mixture into an ungreased 1½-quart, deep ovenproof dish. At this point you can let the casserole cool and refrigerate it up to 1 day, or freeze it.

To serve, if frozen or refrigerated, bring the casserole to room temperature. Preheat the oven to 325°. Dot the potatoes with butter, cover with foil and bake at 325° for 30 minutes. Remove foil and bake for 20 minutes more or until the top is bubbly and crusty.

Variation: You can also stuff the filling back into the potato skins. Reheat at 350° for about 20 minutes or until tops are delicately browned and they are heated through.

Yield: 6 servings.

Old Fashioned Creamed Onions

It isn't a special dinner at our house without creamed onions, and this recipe is one of the best.

> 2 *pounds small boiling onions (or whatever small onions you can find)*
> 1/2 *cup butter*
> 1/2 *cup flour*
> 3 *cups light cream*
> 1 1/2 *cups water from cooking the onions*
> *salt and pepper to taste*
> 1/2 *cup white raisins, walnuts or pecans (optional)*

Peel the onions, place them in a saucepan and cover with salted water. Simmer until just tender. Drain off liquid into a bowl. Set onions and liquid aside separately.

In a medium sauce pan melt the butter. When it foams stir in the flour. Cook gently, stirring, for 2 minutes, then add cream. Cook and stir until thickened. Add 1 1/2 cups of reserved onion liquid. Cook for another few minutes. Add salt and pepper to taste. Add the onions and any optional additions. Serve hot.

Note: You can make this ahead and place it in a double boiler or a 350° oven until warm.

Yield: 8 to 10 servings.

Carrots with Onions and Raisins in Creamy Wine Sauce

The name says it all. Taste it and you'll know why it is a family treasure.

1/4 cup butter
1 pound carrots, cut in 1-inch slices
8 ounces small white onions, peeled
3/4 cup light raisins
1 teaspoon salt
1/4 teaspoon pepper
1/4 to 1/2 teaspoon cayenne pepper
1 teaspoon thyme
1 bay leaf
1/2 cup medium-dry white wine
1/4 cup whipping cream

Melt the butter in a large pan over medium heat. When it stops foaming add carrots, onions and raisins. Cook, stirring, for 4 minutes. Add salt, pepper, cayenne, thyme, bay leaf, and wine. Mix well. Cover the pan and simmer 45 to 50 minutes or until vegetables are just tender; don't let them get too soft. Remove from heat. Discard bay leaf. Stir in the cream and reheat gently for a few minutes. Don't let it boil. Serve hot.

Yield: 6 to 8 servings.

MAIN DISHES

Braised Lamb Shanks

A hearty dish for informal holiday entertaining. Perfect after a day of skiing or hiking in the snow. Serve it with a mound of fluffy rice and a green salad.

        3 Tablespoons salad oil
        6 lamb shanks
           salt and pepper to taste
      1/2 teaspoon oregano
        3 cups water
        1 bay leaf
     1 1/2 cups onion, minced
     1 1/2 cups carrots, diced
      3/4 cup celery, diced
        2 small cloves garlic, minced
        1 Tablespoon flour (or more)
     1 1/2 cups button mushrooms, sautéed in 2 teaspoons butter

Heat oil in a large skillet or dutch oven and brown lamb shanks on all sides. Salt and pepper them well. Add oregano, water, bay leaf, onions, carrots, celery and garlic. Cover and simmer very slowly (or place in a 350° oven) for 2 hours or until tender.

Remove meat from skillet, skim fat from cooking liquid. Mix flour with a little water and stir it in to thicken the sauce slightly. Use more flour if you like a thicker sauce. Return meat to the sauce along with sautéed mushrooms. Simmer for 5 to 10 minutes to heat well and blend the flavors.

Serve the lamb shanks on a bed of hot fluffy rice with a little sauce spooned over them and pass the rest of the sauce.

Note: For an informal supper I often omit the rice and serve lots of crusty French bread to mop up the sauce.

Yield: 6 servings.

Maggie's Individual Roast Chickens

Maggie is one of those hostesses who has little time to spend in the kitchen and yet always entertains elegantly. The chicken breasts, stuffed under the skin, plump up to a luscious golden brown. Serve them with gravy as you would roast chicken. This dish looks very festive.

1   *box (6 ounces) stuffing mix*
1   *egg, slightly beaten*
6   *half chicken breasts with the skin intact*
1   *Tablespoon olive oil (about)*
    salt and pepper
1   *teaspoon dried herb such as thyme, tarragon or oregano*
3   *Tablespoons butter*
1¹/2 *cups chicken stock or water*
¹/4 *cup flour mixed with ¹/2 cup water*
1   *Tablespoon sherry, optional*
    salt and pepper to taste

Preheat oven to 375°.

Prepare stuffing according to package directions, adding a lightly beaten egg. Rub each breast half with olive oil. Sprinkle with salt and pepper and dried herbs. With your fingers, loosen the skin from the breast meat and push one-sixth of the stuffing into the pocket. Pat to make an even, plump layer between skin and meat. Repeat with the remaining breasts. Dot each with butter.

Place in a shallow roasting pan about 1 inch apart and roast at 350° for 35 to 40 minutes. Baste with pan juices after 15 minutes and every 10 minutes thereafter.

Remove breasts to serving platter and keep them warm. Place the roasting pan over a burner over medium heat, pour stock or water into the pan and scrape up all the brown juices with a wooden spoon. Stir in the flour-water mixture and cook and stir until thickened. Taste and add salt and pepper. Add optional sherry, if desired. Spoon a little gravy over each mini-roast. Serve the rest of the gravy separately in a sauce boat. Serve the roasts hot.

Yield: 6 servings.

French Beef Stew with Olives

A wonderful hearty winter stew simmered lovingly until the beef, olives and mushrooms soak up each others's flavors, the sauce cooks down thick and rich, and your house if filled wonderful aromas. Make it ahead and reheat for holiday parties.

3 pounds top round steak
1 Tablespoon vegetable oil
3 Tablespoons butter
3 Tablespoons brandy
3 Tablespoons flour
1 jar (2 ounces) pitted green olives
1 teaspoon tomato paste
2 cups beef stock
1/2 cup dry red wine (or vermouth)
1 bay leaf
1 Tablespoon red currant jelly
8 ounces mushrooms, sautéed in a little butter
3 tomatoes, sliced thin
3 Tablespoons grated Swiss cheese

Remove excess fat from the meat and cut it in 1 or 2 inch chunks. Heat oil and butter in a skillet over medium high heat and brown the meat in batches so as not to crowd the skillet. Remove meat as it browns. Return all meat to the pan, add the brandy and set it aflame. When the flame dies out, remove the meat.

Stir flour into the pan juices, then add olives, tomato paste and beef stock. Mix well and bring to a boil. Add wine, bay leaf, currant jelly and the beef. Cover and simmer for 1½ hours or until tender. Add sautéed mushrooms. If preparing ahead, stop now and refrigerate or freeze.

To finish the dish, reheat and transfer to a deep, ovenproof serving dish. top with sliced tomatoes, sprinkle with cheese and run under the broiler just long enough to heat the tomatoes and melt the cheese. Serve hot with mashed or boiled potatoes.

Note: You can also reheat this dish in the oven at 350°, then top as directed.

Yield: 4 to 6 servings.

Roast Turkey with All the Trimmings

This is how I do my holiday turkey—roasted dark gold and crispy, filled with onion-sage stuffing, and surrounded by a savory mixture of sautéed sausages, mushrooms, pearl onions and chestnuts.

> 1 *14-pound turkey*
> 5 *cups chicken stock*
>   *salt and pepper*
> 2 *Tablespoons butter*

Dressing

> 1 *package (1 pound) Pepperidge Farm® herb seasoned stuffing mix*
> 8 *ounces butter*
> 2 *cups water*
> 1 *cup minced onion*
> 1 *cup minced celery*

Gravy

> 3 *Tablespoons soft butter*
> 3 *Tablespoons flour*

Garnish

> 20 *pieces (1-inch each) breakfast sausage*
> 30 *whole small mushrooms*
>   *butter for sautéing*
> 25 *to 30 small pearl onions (use the smallest ones your market offers)*
> 1 *can (10 ounces) whole chestnuts*
> 1 *Tablespoon butter*

Preheat oven to 375°.

Remove giblets from turkey, set the liver aside for another use and place the heart, gizzard and neck in a large saucepan with 5 cups chicken stock. Heat to boiling, reduce heat and simmer covered for 1 hour. Strain the stock and set it aside. Chop meat from giblets finely and set aside for giblet gravy. (Use the neck meat for sandwiches.)

Wipe turkey dry inside and out with paper towels. Season inside and out with salt and pepper.

To make the dressing, follow package directions (using the butter and water). Add chopped onions and celery. Stuff the turkey loosely with the mixture (place any extra stuffing in a casserole to heat, covered, at 350° for 30 minutes). Truss the turkey and rub the outside with 2 tablespoons butter. Place it breast side up in a shallow roasting pan and roast at 375° until a meat thermometer inserted in the thickest part of the thigh registers 180°, about 2 to 2½ hours. Baste every 15 minutes with the stock. If the turkey begins to brown too quickly, cover it with a tent of aluminum foil.

Place turkey on a serving platter, remove trussing string and let it stand for 25 to 30 minutes so the juices settle back into the meat.

To make gravy, pour grease off the pan drippings. Pour the drippings into a medium-size sauce pan. If you like giblet gravy, add chopped giblets now. Bring the mixture to a boil. In a small bowl cream 3 tablespoons butter with the flour. Gradually stir bits of it into the drippings. Cook and stir until thickens. Thin the mixture with reserved stock to the consistency you like.

To make the garnish, separately fry sausages in a medium skillet. Remove to a large skillet and set aside. In another skillet, sauté mushrooms in butter for 15 minutes. Add to sausages. Sauté onions until golden on all sides. Add 2 tablespoons water, cover, and cook gently until tender and water has evaporated. Add to sausages. Drain chestnuts well. Sauté in one tablespoon butter over medium heat until heated through and add to sausages. Just before serving, reheat garnish.

To serve, heap heated garnish around the turkey. Serve gravy separately.

Serves: 12.

Holiday Seafood Casserole

This is rich and absolutely delicious. Perfect for buffet entertaining or for elegant little holiday suppers.

- 1/4 *cup butter, melted*
- 1/2 *cup chopped scallions*
- 1/4 *cup minced parsley*
- 2 *teaspoons minced garlic*
- 8 *ounces Parmesan cheese, freshly grated*
- 1 *cup mayonnaise*
- 1 *cup sour cream*
- 2 *Tablespoons lemon juice (or more)*
- 1 *pound small shrimp, peeled*
- 1 *(14 ounces) waterpack artichoke hearts, drained and chopped coarsely*
- 1/8 *teaspoon Tabasco®*
  salt and pepper to taste
- 3 *to 4 pounds white fleshed fish, such as sole, flounder, haddock*
  parsley for garnish
- 6 *Tablespoons silvered almonds*

Heat oven to 350°. In a medium skillet melt butter over medium heat. Add scallions, parsley and garlic and sauté, stirring constantly for 5 to 6 minutes. Be careful that the garlic does not burn. Stir in cheese, mayonnaise, sour cream, and lemon juice. Reduce the heat to very low. Stir and cook the mixture for 10 minutes. Remove the skillet from the heat, stir in shrimp and artichokes. Season to taste with Tabasco, salt and pepper.

Cut fish into serving-size pieces and pat dry. Set aside. In the bottom of a greased, ovenproof casserole that will just hold the fish in one layer, make a bed of half the shrimp mixture. Top with all of the fish, making one layer only. Top with remaining shrimp mixture. Sprinkle with parsley for garnish. Bake at 350o for 20 minutes. Remove from oven.

Drain off any liquid that has accumulated. Sprinkle almonds over the top and run the dish under the broiler for a minute or two until the top is golden. Serve hot.

Yield: 8 servings.

Beef Stroganoff

Beef strips in a creamy, mushroom sauce. The perfect buffet dish for an elegant party. It freezes well, reheats well and people love it.

3   *pounds beef round steak*
2   *Tablespoons vegetable oil*
$1/4$ *cup butter*
2   *large onions, chopped fine*
1   *pound fresh mushrooms, sliced*
1   *teaspoon meat glaze (I use Bovril®)*
1   *teaspoon tomato paste*
$1/4$ *cup flour*
2   *cups chicken stock (use 2 bouillon cubes and 2 cups water)*
2   *cups sour cream*
    salt and pepper to taste

Remove fat from the meat and cut it into 2 x ½ inch-fingers, cutting across the grain. Heat a large frying pan very hot. Add the oil and, as soon as it is hot, brown the meat quickly on all sides. Do this in batches if necessary; don't crowd the meat. Remove from pan as it browns and set aside.

Melt the butter in the same pan over medium heat and sauté onions and mushrooms in butter until the onion is transparent. Don't let it brown. Remove from heat and stir in the meat glaze, tomato paste and flour. When smooth, add the chicken stock. Return to the heat and stir until the mixture boils and thickens. Add the meat, cover, turn heat to low and simmer gently for 20 to 30 minutes, or until tender. (If making ahead, freeze at this point.)

Remove from heat and stir in the sour cream. Taste and add salt and pepper. Reheat, but don't let the sauce boil. Serve hot with noodles or fluffy boiled rice.

Yield: 8 servings.

Chicken and Seafood Gumbo

This wonderful gumbo is part soup, part stew—hearty but not too rich; informal but elegant.

16 *chicken thighs or legs*
3 *Tablespoons cooking oil*
3 *Tablespoons butter*
2 *pounds small zucchini, cut in 1/4-inch slices*
4 *medium onions, thinly sliced*
1 *teaspoon minced garlic*
2 *cups ham, diced*
3 *cups canned tomatoes, drained*
2 *cups chicken stock*
1 *large bay leaf*
1 *teaspoon thyme*
1/4 *cup chopped parsley*
1 *pint oysters with their liquid*
1 *pound shrimp, peeled and cooked*
1 *pound crab, cooked*
    salt and pepper to taste
    Tabasco® to taste

Heat a large skillet, add 2 tablespoons each oil and butter and when very hot, brown the chicken pieces.

Remove to a large dutch oven as they brown, adding more oil and butter as needed. In the same fat (add more if needed) sauté zucchini, onions, and garlic until soft. Add to the chicken along with the ham, tomatoes, chicken stock, bayleaf, thyme and parsley. Drain the oyster liquid into the pot, reserving the oysters for later. Cover and simmer very gently for 1 to 1½ hours or until chicken is very tender. If not ready to serve, set aside.

Just before serving add the drained oysters, shrimp and crab. Heat briefly only enough to warm the seafood through. Don't actually cook the seafood or you will toughen it. Taste and add salt, pepper, and enough Tabasco to zap it up.

Serve hot from a large bowl with a dish of fluffy, boiled rice.

Yield: 8 servings.

Turkey-Ham Casserole

Here's wonderful party casserole using the turkey and ham leftover from the holiday feast. It's a perfect dish to welcome guests on a cold night.

1/2 cup onion, chopped
2 Tablespoons butter
3 Tablespoons flour
1/2 teaspoon salt
1/4 teaspoon pepper
1/8 teaspoon cayenne pepper
1/4 teaspoon nutmeg
1 can (3 ounces) sliced mushrooms with their liquid
1 cup table cream or half and half
2 Tablespoons dry sherry
2 cups cooked turkey, cubed
1 cup cooked ham, cubed
1/2 cup sliced canned water chestnuts
1/2 cup sliced almonds
3/4 cup Swiss cheese, shredded
1 cup soft white bread crumbs
2 Tablespoons butter, melted

Preheat oven to 400°.

Cook onions in butter until transparent. Stir in flour, salt, pepper, cayenne and nutmeg. Add mushrooms with their liquid, cream, and sherry and cook until thickened. Stir in the turkey, ham, chestnuts and almonds. Place in a 6-cup casserole and sprinkle with cheese. In a small bowl mix crumbs and butter. Place them around the edge of the casserole. Bake at 400° for 25 minutes or until well heated and lightly browned.

Yield: 6 servings.

Glazed Cornish Game Hens with Wild Rice Stuffing

Succulent little hens glazed with currant jelly and spices, nestled in a bed of nutty wild and brown rice. This dish will make your guests glad they know you.

$2^1/3$	cups chicken stock
$^1/2$	cup wild rice
2	Tablespoons butter
$^1/2$	cup brown rice
3	Tablespoons butter, divided
1	medium onion, chopped
8	ounces small mushrooms, sliced
$^1/4$	cup celery, chopped
$^1/2$	cup pecans, coarsely chopped
2	Tablespoons fresh parsley, chopped
$^1/4$	teaspoon thyme
$^1/4$	teaspoon oregano
	salt and pepper, to taste
4	Cornish game hens
4	Tablespoons butter, softened

Gravy

$^1/2$	cup currant jelly
2	Tablespoons butter
2	Tablespoons fresh lemon juice
$^1/4$	cup red wine vinegar
1	teaspoon salt
3	whole cloves
1	Tablespoon cornstarch mixed with 1 Tablespoon water

In a medium pan bring stock to a boil. Add wild rice and 2 tablespoons butter. Cover and cook over very low heat for 10 minutes. Add the brown rice, cover and continue cooking for 50 minutes more, or until all liquid is absorbed. Add 1 tablespoon butter and fluff with a fork.

Sauté onion, mushrooms and celery in 2 tablespoons butter over medium high heat until onions are transparent and liquid has evaporated. Add to the cooked rice along with pecans, parsley, thyme, oregano and pepper. Cool.

Preheat oven to 350°.

Liberally salt and pepper game hens inside and out, stuff loosely with rice mixture. There will be a good deal left over. Put that in a greased casserole, cover it, and place in the oven with the birds for the last half hour of roasting. Truss the birds, place in a shallow baking pan that just fits but keeps them about an inch apart. Dot each with 1 tablespoon soft butter. Roast at 350° for 30 minutes, then baste every 15 minutes with currant sauce (instructions follow) and continue roasting until hens have baked for a total of 1½ hours. Remove from oven, place on a platter and surround with stuffing from the casserole. Pour the fat off the pan juices. Stir cornstarch-water mixture into the juices and bring to a boil. Cook several minutes, until thickened. Spoon a little sauce over each bird and serve the rest separately.

To make the currant sauce, melt butter with jelly and lemon juice. When jelly has melted, add vinegar, salt and cloves. Bring to a boil and remove from heat.

Yield: 4 servings.

BREADS, PASTRY & CAKES

Cranberry Muffins

Golden, ruby-dotted muffins, their moist sweetness perked up with tart cranberries. Serve them hot from the oven with a bowl of whipped butter to melt into their steamy centers.

- 1 cup cranberries
- 2 Tablespoons sugar
- 2 cups flour
- 1/2 cup sugar
- 3 teaspoons baking powder
- 1/4 teaspoon salt
- 1 cup milk
- 1 teaspoon vanilla
- 1/4 cup butter or margarine, melted
- 2 eggs

Preheat oven to 400°.

Chop the cranberries coarsely, place them in a small bowl, stir in 2 tablespoons of sugar and let them sit for 30 minutes.

In a large bowl mix the flour, sugar, baking powder and salt. In a second bowl beat together milk, vanilla, melted butter and eggs. Add this to the dry ingredients and mix with a few strokes, just to blend. Fold in the cranberries and whatever juice has accumulated.

Fill greased muffin cups 3/4 full and bake at 400° for 20 to 25 minutes.

Yield: 15 to 16 muffins.

Sour Cream Coffee Cake

Moist and tender with a surprise center of raisins, cinnamon and crunchy walnuts. Serve it warm from the oven with coffee and cocoa after the presents are opened.

$1^3/_4$ cups cake flour, sifted
$1^1/_2$ teaspoons baking powder
 $^1/_2$ teaspoon baking soda
 $^1/_2$ cup butter or margarine
$3/_4$ cup sugar
  2   eggs
  1   cup sour cream
  1   teaspoon vanilla
 $^1/_4$ cup sugar
  2   teaspoons cinnamon
 $^1/_2$ cup raisins
 $^1/_2$ cup chopped walnuts or pecans

Preheat oven to 350°.

Sift flour, baking powder and soda into a bowl and set aside. In a medium bowl cream butter and ¾ cup sugar. Add eggs and beat until light and fluffy. Combine sour cream and vanilla. Beat the dry ingredients alternately with the sour cream and vanilla, into the butter-egg mixture, starting and ending with dry ingredients, and using about ⅓ of each at a time. Pour half of the batter into a greased 9-inch bundt pan.

In a small bowl combine ¼ cup sugar, cinnamon, raisins and nuts. Sprinkle half of this over the batter in the pan. Top with the remaining batter and sprinkle with remaining sugar mixture.

Bake at 350° for 45 minutes or until golden.

Yield: 9 to 12 servings.

Orange Date Nut Bread

Make little loaves of this moist orange bread for holiday giving or keep some on hand for breakfast and fireside teas.

       2   medium oranges
       2   cups flour
    $1/2$ cup sugar
       2   teaspoons baking powder
    $1/2$ teaspoon baking soda
    $1/2$ teaspoon salt
       1   cup dates, coarsely chopped
    $3/4$ cup walnuts, coarsely chopped
       1   egg
    $1/2$ cup water
       2   Tablespoons butter, melted and cooled

Preheat oven to 350°.

Peel the oranges, removing all the white pith. Cut in half, pick out the seeds, then quarter them and grind in the blender.

In a large bowl mix flour, sugar, baking powder, baking soda and salt. Toss 1 cup of this with the dates and nuts. In another bowl mix the egg, water, cooled butter and ground oranges. Pour the wet ingredients into the flour-sugar mixture. Stir until barely moistened, then add the date mixture. Blend quickly but thoroughly; never overmix quick breads or they lose their lightness. Pour into two 6x3x2-inch loaf pans and bake at 350° for 30 to 40 minutes or until the top is golden, the edges brown and pulling away from the pan, and a toothpick inserted in the center comes out dry. Cool 10 minutes in the pan, then remove and cool on a rack.

Note: You can also bake this bread in one $8^{1}/2$ x $4^{1}/2$-inch loaf pan at 350° for 60 to 65 minutes or until done.

Yield: 2 small loaves or 1 large loaf.

Mint and Chocolate Pie

Anyone reading this recipe will recognize the frozen mint and chocolate confection generally known as Grasshopper Pie. I don't need to tell you how good it tastes!

16 *chocolate cream sandwich cookies*
1 *Tablespoon butter, melted*
26 *(6 ounces) large marshmallows*
²/₃ *cup milk*
1 *cup whipping cream*
6 *Tablespoons green Crème de Menthe*
2 *Tablespoons white Crème de Cacao*
    candied cherries and candied angelica for garnish

Reduce the cookies to fine crumbs in a blender or food processor. Pour into a bowl, stir in the melted butter and press the mixture into the bottom and up the sides of a 9-inch pie pan.

Place marshmallows and milk in a saucepan and heat over medium heat until marshmallows are melted. Cool the mixture for 30 minutes, or until it starts to thicken slightly. Whip the cream and fold it into the milk mixture along with Crème de Menthe and Crème de Cacao. Pour into the chocolate crust and freeze until firm. Garnish with candied cherries and candied angelica.

Serve frozen, but if it is very hard, remove the pie to the refrigerator for 30 to 60 minutes before serving to soften it slightly. You want a smooth creamy texture.

Note: You can find candied angelica in most gourmet stores or in the specialty section of your supermarket.

Yield: 6 to 8 servings.

Old Fashioned Apple Tart

A Dutch version of apple pie, just made for cold winter days. Serve with a generous topping of unsweetened whipped cream.

1   *9-inch unbaked pie shell*
4   *cups sliced tart pie apples*
1/2 *cup raisins*
1/4 *cup currants*
1/2 *cup slivered almonds*
1   *Tablespoon minced crystallized ginger*
1/2 *cup brown sugar*
1/4 *teaspoon salt*
2   *Tablespoons butter*
1/2 *to 3/4 cup whipping cream, whipped*

Preheat oven to 450°.

In the pie shell, place a layer of apples, raisins, currants, almonds and ginger. Sprinkle with some sugar and salt. Repeat until all these ingredients are used. Dot with butter. Bake on the lower shelf in a 450° oven for 10 minutes. Then reduce the heat to 350° and bake until the apples are puffed and brown, about 30 minutes.

Serve warm with unsweetened, whipped cream.

Yield: 6 servings.

Classic Pumpkin Pie

Without pumpkin pie, there is no holiday season. This is an especially good recipe.

    2   *eggs*
    2   *cups canned pumpkin*
   3/4 *cup brown sugar, firmly packed*
   1/2 *teaspoon salt*
    1   *teaspoon cinnamon*
   1/2 *teaspoon ginger*
   1/4 *teaspoon cloves*
    1   *cup milk*
   2/3 *cup whipping cream*
    1   *9-inch unbaked pie shell*

Preheat oven to 425°.

In the bowl of a food processor or blender jar place eggs, pumpkin, sugar, salt, cinnamon, ginger, cloves, milk and whipping cream. Blend until smooth. Pour into the pie shell. Bake at 425° for 15 minutes. Lower heat to 350° and bake for 45 minutes more or until a knife inserted 1 inch from the edge comes out clean.

Serve at room temperature with or without whipped cream topping.

Variation: If you feel especially festive, you can add 1 tablespoon of brandy to the pumpkin mixture.

Yield: 6 to 8 servings.

Frozen Holiday Log

Wait till you taste this cake roll filled with pecan caramel cream and iced with the requisite oh-so-rich chocolate.

1 cup heavy cream
1/4 cup firmly packed dark brown sugar
1/2 cup pecans, chopped
1 Tablespoon butter
1 cup sifted cake flour
1 teaspoon baking powder
1/4 teaspoon salt
3 eggs
1 cup granulated sugar
1/3 cup water
1 teaspoon vanilla
confectioners sugar

Frosting

1 cup heavy cream
1 1/4 cups sugar
5 squares (1 ounce each) unsweetened chocolate in small pieces
1/2 cup butter
1 teaspoon vanilla

Mix heavy cream and brown sugar; chill for 1 hour. Brown nuts lightly in butter and drain on paper towel. Reserve.

Preheat oven to 375°. Grease a jelly roll pan (10 1/2 x 15 1/2 inches). Line it with waxed paper cut long enough to extend an inch beyond the two short sides. Grease and flour the paper. Sift flour with baking powder and salt and set aside. In a medium bowl beat eggs until very thick and light colored, then gradually beat in sugar. Blend in water and vanilla. Add flour mixture and beat until smooth.

Pour batter into prepared pan and bake at 375° for 12 to 13 minutes. (Don't overbake. An overbaked cake is tough and the paper is hard to remove.) The edge of the cake should just begin to color. Sprinkle a clean dish towel with confectioners sugar. Using a small knife, loosen the sides of the cake from the pan and invert it onto the towel. Peel off the paper and cut off the crisp edges. Roll up the cake in the towel from the narrow end, making a short, fat roll, and place it on a rack to cool (about 20 to 30 minutes).

Whip the reserved sugared cream until stiff and fold in the toasted nuts. Unroll the cake and spread with the cream mixture, keeping the cream about ½ inch from the edges. Roll up the cake (without the towel, of course). It isn't always easy to keep the cream evenly inside. When you have about 6 inches of unrolled cake left, flip up that side, using the towel to help you. Place cake seam-down on a platter, wrap and freeze. The cake will keep well for 3 to 4 weeks.

On serving day, make the frosting. In a large, heavy saucepan stir heavy cream and sugar to mix well, then heat to a boil over medium, stirring constantly. Reduce the heat and simmer for precisely 6 minutes. Immediately remove the pan from the heat and stir in the chocolate pieces. When they are melted stir in the butter and vanilla.

Set the pan in a bowl filled with ice cubes and water and stir frequently while the frosting cools (8 to 10 minutes). When it begins to thicken, remove from the ice water and beat with a wooden spoon until it is spreading consistency (about 3 minutes).

Remove cake from freezer, unwrap and place on your serving plate. Frost top and sides. With a fork, make lengthwise markings to resemble bark. Return to the freezer.

About 20 minutes before serving, place the Holiday Log at room temperature to soften the filling. Decorate with tiny branches of evergreen, maybe a little holly, and a flurry of confectioners sugar snow.

Note: Leftover cake will keep for one month in the freezer.

Yield: 10 servings.

Caramel-Topped Spice Cake

This tall, moist cake topped with rich, fluffy caramel icing pleases everyone.

     2   cups flour
  1 1/2   cups sugar
     3   teaspoons baking powder
     1   teaspoon salt
   1/2   teaspoon allspice
   1/2   teaspoon cloves
     1   teaspoon cinnamon
   1/2   teaspoon nutmeg
     7   eggs, separated
   1/2   cup cooking oil
   3/4   cup ice water
     1   teaspoon grated lemon rind
   1/2   teaspoon cream of tartar

Frosting
   1/2   cup butter
  2 1/2   Tablespoons flour
   1/4   teaspoon salt
   1/2   cup milk
   1/2   cup firmly backed light brown sugar
     2   cups confectioners sugar
     1   teaspoon vanilla
     1   cup chopped pecans

Preheat oven to 325°.

Into a large bowl sift flour, sugar, baking powder, salt, allspice, cloves, cinnamon and nutmeg: In the large bowl of your mixer beat egg yolks, oil and water to combine. Add the sifted dry ingredients and lemon rind and beat for half a minute on low speed. In a large bowl beat egg whites and cream of tartar until stiff but not dry. Gently fold them into the batter.

Pour into an ungreased 10-inch tube pan and bake at 325° for 55 minutes. Raise oven heat to 350° and bake for 10 to 15 minutes more. Remove from oven. Invert the pan to cool. (If your pan doesn't have a raised center tube to rest on, place it upside down over a narrow-necked tall bottle.) When cake is completely cool, remove from pan and frost.

To make frosting, in a saucepan blend butter, flour and salt and cook for 1 minute. Don't let the butter brown. Stir in milk and cook, stirring, until thickened and smooth. Remove from heat and beat in the brown sugar. Cool the mixture to lukewarm and beat in confectioners sugar. When thick and creamy stir in vanilla and nuts.

Yield: 1 10-inch cake.

Southern Chess Tarts

These heavenly little chewy date-nut tarts, with a hint of brandy, are a staple in our house. Keep a batch in the freezer; they thaw in minutes.

> 1   cup sugar
> 1/2 cup softened butter
> 1   cup walnuts, chopped
> 1   cup dates, chopped
> 2   eggs, slightly beaten
> 1   Tablespoon vanilla
> 6   Tablespoons whipping cream
> 2   Tablespoons brandy
> 24 pastry-lined muffin cups (you need dough from 2 9-inch crusts)

Preheat oven to 400°.

Place sugar, butter, walnuts, dates, eggs, vanilla, whipping cream and brandy in a large bowl and mix, chopping down with the spoon to break up the butter, until all is well mixed, but some of the butter remains in tiny pieces. Fill pastry-lined muffin cups ⅔ full and bake at 400° for 10 to 15 minutes. Remove tarts from the pans while hot or they will stick. If they do stick, just slip them back in the oven for a few seconds to soften the sugar (that's what's sticking).

Yield: 24 tarts.

Baked Cranberry Pudding

An old fashioned pudding, filled with cranberries, and topped with a dreamy cranberry glaze. Serve it warm, elegant with whipped cream, or homey in bowls with fluid cream. This pudding says there's a Mom or a Grandma in the house; it's that sort of wonderful.

2	*eggs, separated*
1	*cup light brown sugar, firmly packed*
1/2	*cup whipping cream*
2	*teaspoons vanilla*
1/2	*teaspoon nutmeg*
1	*teaspoon cinnamon*
1 1/2	*cups flour*
1/2	*teaspoon cream of tartar, divided*
1	*teaspoon baking powder*
1/8	*teaspoon salt*
	grated peel of 1 orange
3	*cups cranberries, coarsely chopped*
1/4	*cup butter, melted*
1 1/2	*cups granulated sugar*
1/2	*cup orange juice*
2 1/2	*cups whole cranberries*
1	*cup whipping cream*
2	*Tablespoons confectioners sugar*

Preheat oven to 350°.

In a medium bowl mix egg yolks with brown sugar. Stir in whipping cream, vanilla, nutmeg and cinnamon and set aside.

In a large bowl mix flour, 1/4 teaspoon cream of tartar, baking powder, salt and orange peel. Add chopped cranberries and mix well to coat completely. Stir in the cream mixture and melted butter and mix to a stiff batter.

In a medium bowl beat the egg whites until they start to thicken, add 1/4 teaspoon cream of tartar and beat to soft peaks. Fold into batter and pour into a greased springform pan, 9 inches in diameter and 3 inches deep or 9½ inches in diameter and 2 inches deep. (A standard 9-inch layer pan is not deep enough.) Place pan on a baking sheet and bake at 350° for 30 to 35 minutes or until the top springs back when lightly pressed.

While the pudding bakes bring sugar and orange juice to a boil over medium heat, stirring. Boil for about 3 minutes, or until the sugar has melted, then add the whole cranberries and cook and stir over low heat, for 5 to 8 minutes or until berries are shimmering and most have split. Keep warm.

When the pudding is done, spoon the hot cranberry mixture over the top in an even layer and return to the 350° oven for another 10 minutes. Remove from oven. Cool at room temperature for at least 1 hour before serving. The pudding can wait overnight, covered with plastic, at room temperature. To serve, reheat uncovered at 350° for 10 to 15 minutes.

Whip cream with confectioners sugar and spoon it around the edges of the pudding or pipe it on with a pastry bag, leaving the bright red center exposed. Do this just before serving because the pudding is warm and the cream will soften quickly. Or serve the whipped cream separately. For informal, homespun occasions, serve the pudding in ceramic bowls with plenty of cream to pour over the top.

Yield: 8 to 10 servings.

COOKIES

Holiday Cherry Bonbons

Bite through crisp, buttery, cream cheese dough to find an almond covered cherry with a tiny chocolate heart. Very special.

 6 *ounces cream cheese, room temperature*
 3/4 cup butter, room temperature
 1 1/2 cups flour
 1 *jar (10 ounces) maraschino cherries, well drained*
 4 *Tablespoons chocolate chips*
 3/4 cup confectioners sugar
 8 *ounces almond paste*
   confectioners sugar

In a medium bowl mix cream cheese and butter until fluffy. Stir in the flour to make a stiff dough. Gather into a ball, wrap, and chill in the refrigerator for 2 hours or in the freezer for 45 minutes.

Preheat oven to 375°.

Push a chocolate chip inside each well drained cherry. Pinch off a small amount of almond paste, flatten it, and wrap it around each cherry.

Generously coat your work surface with confectioners sugar (the dough will probably absorb about 1/2 cup), and roll out the dough 1/8-inch thick. Cut in 3-inch rounds. Completely enclose a wrapped cherry in each, pinch well to seal and place, sealed side down, on a baking sheet. Bake at 375° for 16 to 18 minutes, or until lightly golden. Remove from oven and while still hot, sprinkle with more confectioners sugar. Cool the cookies on a rack.

Note: Almond paste is available at most supermarkets and gourmet stores.

Yield: about 3 dozen.

Butterscotch Brownies

These chewy squares ooze brown sugary butterscotch. They becrumb the lips and besmear the chin, like home-baked holiday goodies should.

1 cup butter, melted
2 cups light brown sugar
3 eggs
2 teaspoons vanilla
2 cups flour
$1/2$ teaspoon salt
$1^1/2$ teaspoons baking powder
1 cup chopped nuts (walnuts, pecans, whatever)

Frosting

$1/2$ cup butter
3 cups sifted confectioners sugar
2 teaspoons instant coffee dissolved in 2 Tablespoons hot
water

Preheat oven to 350°.

Melt butter in a large saucepan. Add sugar and beat well to mix. Cool the mixture slightly, then beat in the eggs and vanilla.

Sift together flour, salt and baking powder. Stir it into the wet ingredients, then add the nuts. Mix well. Spread brownies in a greased 11x7x2-inch pan and bake at 350° for 30 to 35 minutes or until a light gold. Cool in the pan for 10 minutes, then turn out. This is easiest if you up-end the pan over waxed paper, then turn the cake right side up. Let it finish cooling on a rack.

To make the frosting, cream ½ cup butter with confectioners sugar. Beat it until light, then beat in the coffee mixture. Spread over the brownies. When frosting has set, cut in squares.

Yield: 3 dozen 2-inch or 6 dozen 1-inch squares.

Rocky Road Bars

These are delicious for an open house or informal party.

- 1/2 cup butter
- 1 square (1 ounce) unsweetened chocolate
- 1 cup sugar
- 1 cup flour
- 1 teaspoon baking powder
- 1 cup chopped nuts
- 1 teaspoon vanilla
- 2 eggs, lightly beaten

Cream Cheese Filling

- 6 ounces cream cheese, room temperature
- 1/4 to 1/2 cup sugar
- 2 Tablespoons flour
- 1/4 cup butter, softened
- 1 egg
- 1/2 teaspoon vanilla
- 1/4 cup chopped nuts
- 1 cup semisweet chocolate chips
- 2 cups miniature marshmallows

Frosting

- 1/4 cup butter
- 1 (1 ounce) square unsweetened chocolate
- 2 ounces cream cheese, softened
- 1/4 cup milk
- 1 box (1 pound) confectioners sugar
- 1 teaspoon vanilla

Preheat oven to 350°.

In a medium sauce pan, over low heat, melt butter and chocolate. Remove from heat and stir in sugar. Mix flour with baking powder and nuts and add to the chocolate-sugar mixture along with the vanilla and eggs. Spread in a greased and floured 13x9-inch baking pan. Set aside while you make the filling.

Beat cream cheese, sugar, flour, butter, egg and vanilla until smooth and fluffy. Stir in nuts. Spread this filling over the chocolate batter.

Sprinkle with chocolate chips and bake at 350° for 20 to 25 minutes or until it tests done with a toothpick. Remove from the oven, sprinkle with marshmallows and bake for 2 minutes more.

Make the frosting while the bars bake. In a medium saucepan, melt butter over low heat. Stir in chocolate, cream cheese and milk. Heat gently, stirring, just until smooth. Remove from heat. Beat in confectioners sugar and vanilla. As soon as you remove the pan from the oven, spread on the frosting, swirling it into the marshmallows. Cool on a rack and cut into bars. These improve if you refrigerate them for a few hours.

Yield: 36 bars

Pecan Crispies

Wonderful, chewy cookies to delight your family when they come home all rosy cheeked and ravenous.

$^1/_2$ cup butter, room temperature
$^1/_2$ cup solid vegetable shortening
$2^1/_2$ cups light brown sugar, firmly packed
2 eggs, slightly beaten
$2^1/_2$ cups sifted flour
$^1/_2$ teaspoon baking soda
$^1/_4$ teaspoon salt
1 cup chopped pecans

Preheat oven to 350°.

In a large mixing bowl cream butter, shortening and sugar until light. Add eggs one at a time, beating well after each addition. Sift together flour, soda, and salt and add to the creamed mixture. Stir in the pecans.

Drop by heaped teaspoonfuls, 2 inches apart, on a greased baking sheet. Bake at 350° for 12 to 15 minutes or until lightly browned. Don't overbake if you want them a little chewy.

Yield: 5 dozen.

Thumb Print Cookies

A traditional German cookie, crumbly and rich with butter, ground nuts and spices, and topped with a bright raspberry jam center.

    1/2   (scant) cup hazelnuts, blanched and peeled
    1/2   (scant) cup almonds, blanched and peeled
    2   Tablespoons sugar
    1/2   cup butter, room temperature
    6   Tablespoons sugar
    1   egg yolk
    1   teaspoon grated lemon peel
    1   Tablespoon fresh lemon juice
    1   cup flour
    1   teaspoon cinnamon
    1/4   teaspoon cloves
    1   cup raspberry jam (or any tart jam)

Place nuts and 2 tablespoons of sugar in blender or processor bowl and grind until they are like fine dry bread crumbs. Set aside.

In a medium bowl cream butter and sugar until fluffy. Beat in egg yolk, lemon peel and lemon juice. Stir flour, cinnamon, and cloves into the sugar-nut mixture and add, mixing gently but completely. Wrap the dough in plastic wrap and refrigerate for 1 hour or until firm enough to handle.

Preheat oven to 375°.

Form generous teaspoonfuls of dough into 1-inch balls and place them 2 inches apart on an ungreased baking sheet. Dent the top of each with your finger. Bake at 375° for 10 to 12 minutes or until lightly browned on the bottom and barely firm to the touch. Cool on a rack and then fill the dents with jam.

Note: To skin nuts, plunge them into boiling water for 5 to 8 minutes, drain and pinch off the skins.

Yield: 4 dozen.

Holiday Brownie Mints

Luscious brownies topped with soft mint cream, then glazed with chocolate.

2 squares (1 ounce each) unsweetened chocolate
$^1/_2$ cup butter
2 eggs
1 cup sugar
$^1/_2$ teaspoon mint extract
$^1/_2$ cup flour
  pinch salt
3 Tablespoons soft butter
1 cup confectioners sugar
2 Tablespoons whipping cream
1 teaspoon mint extract
  green vegetable coloring
2 squares (1 ounce each) unsweetened chocolate
2 Tablespoons butter

Preheat oven to 350°.

In a small pot, over very low heat melt chocolate with butter. Set aside to cool to lukewarm.

In a mixing bowl beat the eggs. Beat in the sugar, then the cooled chocolate mixture. Add $^1/_2$ teaspoon mint extract, the flour and salt. Mix well. Pour into a greased 9 x 9-inch pan. Bake at 350° for 20 to 25 minutes. Don't overbake; proper brownies are moist and should be more springy to the touch than a cake. Cool in the pan.

For the mint topping, mix 3 tablespoons softened butter with confectioners sugar, whipping cream and 1 teaspoon mint extract. Tint it pale green with vegetable coloring and spread over the cooled brownies. Chill in the refrigerator until firm.

For the glaze, in a small pot over low heat, melt together chocolate and butter. Spread over the chilled green layer and return to the refrigerator to set the glaze. Cut in small squares and serve at room temperature.

Yield: 64 tiny pieces (cutting 8 x 8) or 49 medium ones (cutting 7 x 7).

Meltaway Butter Spirals and Checkerboards

Perhaps the most seductive little rascals in the whole cookie collection. These crunchy, buttery, vanilla-chocolate mosaics melt in the mouth, tempting you to eat more and more.

Vanilla Dough

    1   cup butter, softened
    1   cup sugar
    1   egg plus 1 egg yolk (reserve egg white from second egg)
    1   teaspoon vanilla
    2   cups unsifted flour
    1/2 teaspoon salt

Chocolate Dough

    1   cup butter, softened
    1   cup sugar
    1   egg plus 1 egg yolk (reserve egg white from second egg)
    1   teaspoon vanilla
    1³/4 cups unsifted flour
    1/2 cup cocoa

For Finishing

    2   reserved egg whites

Make the vanilla dough by creaming butter and sugar until fluffy. Beat in egg, egg yolk and vanilla. Add flour and salt gradually to the butter mixture. The dough will be stiff. Form into a flat cake, wrap, and chill 2 hours in the refrigerator or 45 minutes in the freezer.

Make the chocolate dough the same way, adding cocoa with the flour and salt. Chill as above.

Meltaway Spiral Cookies

Preheat oven to 375°.

Roll vanilla dough on floured waxed paper into a rectangle ¼ inch thick, about 7 inches wide and 14 inches long. Do the same with the chocolate dough. In a small bowl, lightly beat the 2 egg whites with a fork and brush it on the vanilla dough to coat completely. Using the waxed paper to help lift, flip the chocolate dough on top of the vanilla. Peel of the paper and roll gently across the top with a rolling pin to seal the layers. Cut edges even with a sharp knife. Paint the chocolate dough with egg white. Starting with a long edge, and using the waxed paper to aid you, roll up the dough. Wrap it and chill for 2 hours in the refrigerator or 45 minutes in the freezer.

You now have a roll of refrigerator cookies which can be sliced and baked whenever you need them. To bake, lay the roll seam down and slice ¼ inch thick with a sharp knife, using a light, sawing motion. Place 1 inch apart on a baking sheet and bake at 375° for 8 to 10 minutes or until the cookies feel firm to the touch. Cool on a wire rack.

Yield: 3 dozen.

Checkerboard Meltaways

Preheat oven to 375°.

Cut each of the chilled doughs into thirds. Put away one piece of the chocolate dough to use any way you like. Form two pieces of each dough into 1-inch thick logs of identical length. Lightly beat the egg white and paint all surfaces. Now lay 1 vanilla and 1 chocolate log on your work surface side by side. Top the vanilla log with a chocolate log, and the chocolate log with a vanilla log. Press all together gently. On floured waxed paper roll the reserved vanilla dough to a rectangle exactly as long as the logs and 4 times as wide. Paint the dough with egg white, then carefully lay the log down the center and, using the paper to help you, fold the vanilla dough around it, making a rim for the checkerboards. Chill roll for 2 hours in the refrigerator or 45 minutes in the freezer.

To bake, lay the seam down and slice ¼-inch thick with a sharp knife, using a light, sawing motion. Place 1 inch apart on a baking sheet and bake at 375° for 8 to 10 minutes or until the cookies feel firm to the touch. Cool on a wire rack.

Yield: about 30.

Chewy Meringue Crescents

With their slightly soft almond centers lurking beneath a coat of crisp nuts these cookies lie on the plate whispering "Eat me." An you will. And you will never regret it; in fact, you will reach for a second and a third.

> 8 ounces almonds (about 1¹/₂ cups), skins removed
> ¹/₄ cup confectioners sugar
> 2 egg whites, lightly beaten
> 1 cup confectioners sugar
> 1 Tablespoon apricot jam
> ¹/₄ teaspoon almond extract
> 4 to 5 ounces (³/₄ to 1 cup) almonds, chopped medium fine
>   confectioners sugar for dusting baked cookies.

In a processor or blender finely grind nuts and 1/4 cup sugar. In a small bowl beat the egg whites with a fork until foamy, and set aside 1 tablespoonful for later use.

In a medium bowl mix ground nuts and 1 cup sugar. Make a well in the center, into it put the jam, almond extract and one third of the egg whites. Mix this gradually into the nuts using a wooden spoon. You want to achieve a mixture that just holds together, so when the first egg white is completely incorporated, dribble in a little more. Mix. (You probably will not need all the egg white.) When the dough starts to hold together, gather it with your hands and knead gently. Dampen any dry bits remaining in the bowl with a bit of egg white and work them in. If the dough is too crumbly, knead in a smidgen of egg white; if too wet, add a bit more sugar.

Preheat oven to 375°.

Roll walnut-size pieces of dough into 3-inch logs. In a small flat dish, lightly beat remaining egg white along with reserved tablespoon of egg white, using a fork. Place chopped nuts on a plate. Roll each log first in egg white, then in nuts. Pinch logs into crescents, place on a baking sheet and bake at 375° for 10 to 12 minutes or until pale gold. Remove from the oven and sprinkle with confectioners sugar.

Note: To skin almonds, plunge into boiling water for 5 to 8 minutes, drain and pinch off the skins.

Yield: 24.

Chinese New Year Cookies

A great, no-bake holiday favorite of my mother. Crunchy, yet chewy, sweet with a smidgen of salt, they vanish at an alarming rate, so make plenty.

    1 can (7¹/4 ounces) salted peanuts
    2 packages (6 ounces each) caramel pieces
    1 can (3 ounces) Chinese noodles

Split the peanuts into halves. In a small pot over boiling water, melt the caramels. Stir in Chinese noodles and peanuts. Drop by teaspoonfuls onto a waxed paper-lined baking sheet and chill until firm. That's all there is to it!

Yield: 30 to 36.

Chocolate Diamonds

Every holiday cookie plate needs some of these. Crispy, chocolaty and nutty.

    1   square (1 ounce) unsweetened chocolate
    ¹/4 cup butter
    ¹/2 cup sugar
    1   egg
    ¹/4 cup flour
    ¹/4 teaspoon vanilla
    ¹/8 teaspoon salt
    ¹/3 cup finely chopped walnuts or pecans

Preheat oven to 400°.

In a medium size pan over hot water or in a double boiler, melt the chocolate and butter. Remove form heat. Beat in sugar, egg, flour, vanilla and salt. The batter will be thin. Divide batter in half and spread it in two greased 8x8x2-inch pans. Sprinkle each with half of the nuts.

Bake at 400° for 12 minutes. Cool slightly, then while in the pan and still warm, cut into 1¹/2-inch diamonds. When cookies are cool, remove from pan and store in tightly covered container.

Yield: 4¹/2 to 5 dozen.

Fruitcake Cookies

A very little bit of spicy dough binds a luxurious assortment of candied fruits and nuts in this perfect holiday cookie. Even fruitcake haters will reach for seconds.

 1   cup candied cherries
 2   cups seedless light raisins
 2   slices candied pineapple
 1/2 cup chopped candied citron
 3   cups pecans
 1/4 cup butter
 1/2 cup brown sugar
 2   eggs
 2   Tablespoons milk
 1/4 cup dry sherry (or white vermouth)
 1 1/2 cups flour
 1 1/2 teaspoons baking soda
 1/2 teaspoon allspice
 1/2 teaspoon cloves
 1/2 teaspoon nutmeg

Preheat oven to 250°; these are baked in a very slow oven.

Chop fruits and nuts medium fine and set aside.

In a medium bowl cream butter and sugar until fluffy. Stir in eggs, milk and wine. Mix well.

Sift flour with baking soda, allspice, cloves and nutmeg. Add half of this to the creamed mixture, mixing well. Blend the other half with the fruits and nuts; then stir them into the batter.

Drop the mixture in 2-tablespoon size mounds on an ungreased cookie sheet, 2-inches apart. Wet your fingers or the back of a spoon and flatten the top of each cookie. Keep the cookie round. Bake at 250° for 30 to 35 minutes or until edges are browned but the top is still moist.

Yield: 3 dozen.

CANDY

Old Faithful Marshmallow Cream Fudge

When I was a kid everybody's mother made this candy—probably because it was so easy and we kids adored it. The recipe still produces a frazzle-free fudgemaker, and a bevy of chocolaty smiles.

$1^2/3$ cups evaporated milk (not condensed)
$3^1/2$ cups sugar
   3   cups (18 ounces) chocolate chips
$^1/2$ cup butter
   1   jar (7 ounces) marshmallow cream
   1   Tablespoon vanilla
$1^1/2$ cups chopped nuts (optional)

In a 3-quart saucepan combine evaporated milk and sugar. Bring to a full, rolling boil over medium high heat, stirring constantly; then keep it boiling and stir vigorously for 9 minutes.

Remove from heat and beat in chocolate chips. When they are melted, stir in butter, marshmallow cream and vanilla (and nuts if you're using them). Mix well.

Pour the fudge into a pan to cool. (I use one 8x8x2 inches, but choose a size that gives the thickness you like your fudge to be.) Chill until set and cut in squares.

Yield: about 2 pounds.

Marzipan

When we lived in Belgium, the arrival of marzipan in the pastry shops each year heralded the start of the holiday season. In our neighborhood the traditional marzipan pig, pink and fat and about 18 inches long, sat atop the glass pastry case. One could buy slices, and as the season progressed, he became shorter and shorter until, like the Cheshire cat, only his grin remained. Somehow, I preferred the tiny fruits temptingly heaped on the glass shelf below.

> 1 cup almond paste
> 1 egg white
> 1 to 1½ cups confectioners sugar
> few drops rose water, orange flower water or lemon juice
> liquid food coloring
> 1 to 2 Tablespoons gin

In a bowl, mash the almond paste to soften it slightly. Separately beat the egg white until fluffy and work it into the paste. Add 1 cup sugar and 1 or 2 drops flavoring. Work until you have a dough you can handle. If it is too sticky, add more sugar; if too dry and crumbly, a few drops lemon juice (the rose water or orange flower water will impart too strong a flavor if added at this point). Then knead until you have a smooth "modeling clay."

Pinch off small balls (about ½ teaspoon) and shape tiny fruits— bananas, apples, pears, oranges, peaches. You can even do little bunches of grapes. Use your imagination.

To color them, in a very small dish or bottle cap, mix 1 or 2 drops of each food coloring with 1 teaspoon of gin. You will probably need yellow, red, orange, brown and green. Pat color on the fruit with a little wad of cotton or cotton swab. They look best when you don't color them completely. Try using several colors (separate cotton for each) on a fruit, such as yellow, red and a hint of green on an apple or peach.

Dry the finished fruits for several hours at room temperature, then store them in an airtight container in the refrigerator.

Yield: about 4 dozen.

Spiced Nuts

These are delicious with drinks or as part of any holiday spread. Keep a bowl in the living room to welcome droppers-in.

> 6   ounces (1¹/2 cups) walnut or pecan halves
> ¹/2 cup sugar
> ¹/4 cup water
> ¹/2 teaspoon grated orange peel
> ¹/4 teaspoon cinnamon
> ¹/8 teaspoon ginger
> ¹/8 teaspoon cloves
>   pinch nutmeg

In a heavy medium-size skillet place nuts, sugar, water, orange peel, cinnamon, ginger, cloves and nutmeg. Bring to a boil over medium high heat and cook gently until the liquid evaporates, leaving the nuts well coated and sugary looking—about 5 minutes. Turn them onto a lightly greased (I use vegetable spray) surface and, while still warm, break them apart with your fingers. Cool before serving.

Yield: 1¹/2 cups.

Chocolate Truffles

Everyone has a favorite recipe for this velvety confection. This is mine.

8 ounces (1¹/₃ cups) chocolate chips
2 Tablespoons whipping cream
2 Tablespoons Bailey's Irish Cream® (or brandy or rum)
¹/₄ cup butter
²/₃ cup confectioners sugar
2 egg yolks
1 teaspoon vanilla
¹/₃ cup coarsely ground hazelnuts (ground in blender)
¹/₂ cup cocoa
¹/₄ cup confectioners sugar
¹/₂ teaspoon cinnamon

In the top of a double boiler over barely simmering water, heat chocolate, whipping cream, liqueur and butter. When the chocolate starts to soften, lift pan off the hot water, and stir until chocolate has softened completely and the mixture is smooth. Place sugar on top and the egg yolks on the sugar (to insulate them from the heat). Quickly stir this into the chocolate. Place over simmering water again and cook, stirring, about 2 minutes or until the chocolate begins to thicken.

Remove from water and beat in vanilla. Stir in hazelnuts. Pour into a shallow dish, cover and chill until you can handle the mixture easily.

In a small, flat dish mix cocoa, sugar, and cinnamon. When chocolate has set, cut it into squares, butter your fingers, and roll it into small balls a little less than an inch in diameter. Roll the balls in the cocoa mixture. Store the truffles covered in the refrigerator. Serve them in paper candy cups. Truffles should be kept in the refrigerator but served at room temperature.

Truffled Pecans: Spread ¹/₄ inch of truffle mixture between 2 pecan halves. Coat exposed chocolate with cocoa-sugar mixture.

Yield: about 6 dozen.

BEVERAGES

Viennese Spiced Coffee

A delicious treat for family or friends who drop in.

- $^1/_3$ cup instant coffee powder
- 3   Tablespoons sugar
- 8   whole cloves
- 1   3-inch stick cinnamon
- $3^1/_2$ cups water
- $^1/_4$ to $^1/_2$ cup whipping cream, whipped
    ground cinnamon
- 4   cinnamon sticks (optional)

In a saucepan combine coffee powder, sugar, spices and water. Bring to a boil. Remove from heat and let it stand, covered, for five minutes to steep. Strain the mixture and pour into cups. Top each serving with whipped cream and a sprinkle of cinnamon. To add a festive touch, add a cinnamon stick to each cup.

Yield: 4 servings.

Holiday Glögg

A wonderful, hot wine punch that fills the house glorious aromas of orange and cinnamon and wine; and fills your guests with holiday contentment.

  9 *large oranges, peels only*
 20 *cardamom pods*
 10 *whole cloves*
  6 *sticks (3-inch size) cinnamon*
  2 *fifths (6 cups) red wine*
  2 *fifths (6 cups) port wine*
  2 *cups blanched almonds*
  2 *cups seedless dark raisins*
  1 *pound sugar cubes*
     a double layer of clean cheesecloth, about 8 or 9 inches square

Peel the oranges thinly with a vegetable peeler, leaving behind as much white pith as you can. Remove the seeds form the cardamom pods and crush them. Place the orange peel, crushed cardamom seeds, cloves and cinnamon sticks in the cheesecloth and tie it securely.

Place the bag of seasonings in a large, heavy pot along with the wine, port, almonds, raisins and sugar. Cover the pot and, over low heat, bring the mixture slowly to a boil. When it just reaches a boil, stir it, remove from the heat, cover and let the glögg stand for at least 24 hours to mellow the flavor.

Just before serving, reheat the glögg. Again, do not let it boil. Remove the spice bag and pour glögg into a punch bowl or just ladle it into cups in the kitchen.

Yield: 24 5-ounce servings.

Holiday Punch

This is an especially good non-alcoholic punch—the sort that both kids and adults enjoy. The orange ice ring looks festive and gives the punch a needed tartness.

    2   cans (30-ounces each) fruit salad in syrup
  2¹/2   cups ginger ale
    1   to 2 Tablespoons lemon juice
    1   frozen ring-mold of orange juice

Puree the fruit salad in the blender, juice and all. Place it in a large, covered container and refrigerate. Just before serving add the ginger ale and 1 tablespoon of lemon juice. Taste and add more lemon juice if needed.

Place orange juice into a ring-mold and freeze until firm. Place the ice ring in your punch bowl and pour in the punch.

Note: Instead of a ring, freeze orange juice in an ice cube tray and put the cubes in the punch. To make it festive, freeze a cherry or mint leaf in each cube.

Yield: 25 to 30 punch-cup servings.

Creamy Eggnog

What is the holiday season without the eggnog? This one is gloriously creamy, slightly sweet, and not too heavily spiked in deference to guests who find that it goes down easily and indulge in several cups. A friend omits the milk and serves the eggnog in champagne or sherbet glasses as a devastating holiday dessert.

6   eggs, separated
2/3   cup granulated sugar
1/2   bourbon whiskey
1/2   cup cognac
1   cup milk
1/4   teaspoon salt
2   cups whipping cream
     grated nutmeg

In the medium bowl of the electric mixer beat egg yolks with sugar until very thick and lemon colored. At low speed, beat in bourbon, cognac and milk. Chill at least 2 to 3 hours.

In a medium bowl beat egg whites and salt semi-stiff; the peaks should flop over very softly instead of standing up. In a medium bowl beat cream stiff.

Fold whipping cream into egg yolks, then fold in egg whites. Chill for 1 hour.

Serve in small punch cups, each serving sprinkled with nutmeg.
Yield: 20 punch-cup servings.